EASY PIANO TUNES

Anthony Marks

Edited by Jenny Tyler
Designed by Doriana Berkovic

Illustrated by Simone Abel
and Kim Blundell

Music selected, arranged and edited by Anthony Marks
New compositions by Anthony Marks
Piano advisor: John York
Music setting: Andrew Jones
Managing designer: Russell Punter

About this book

You will already know some of these tunes, though others might be less familiar. Three of them were written specially for this book. If you have a computer, you can listen to all the tunes on the Usborne Quicklinks Website to hear how they go. Just go to **www.usborne-quicklinks.com** and enter the keywords "easy piano tunes", then follow the simple instructions.

At the top of every piece there is a picture in a circle. Each of these has a sticker to match in the middle of the book. Use these to show that you have learned the piece. There are star stickers too, to use if you or your teacher think you play a piece very well.

Contents

Donkey riding

Although this tune is most popular in Canada, it may have first been sung by French sailors in the 18th century.

Allegro

You could accompany this tune with a drum or shaker, using the rhythms on the right. Which one do you like best? Do you like the same one all the way through?

3

Land of the silver birch

Play this tune quite lightly. Make
sure you don't rush the short notes.
This is another Canadian tune.

Sitting in the sun

This tune was written specially for this book. Watch out for the accidentals and the 2/4 bar.

Golden slumbers

This old English lullaby was first sung in the 15th century. Play it very gently, but not too slowly.

You could ask someone else to join in with this tune. They can play the music below on the violin, keyboard, guitar, chime bars or recorder. (You could copy this out to make it easier to read.)

Someone who plays the cello could play the same notes as the left hand of the piano. Before you begin playing, count a few bars together so that everybody starts at the same time.

The ash grove

"The ash grove" is a very old Welsh tune. Watch out for the repeats, and don't rush the short notes.

Oh my darling Clementine

This American song was written by
Percy Montross around 1880. You can
read some of the words below.

Here are some of the words to
the song. It is about a gold-
miner's family. In the late 1840s,
gold was discovered in
California. In 1849, thousands of
Americans moved there,
hoping to find gold. They were
called "forty-niners".

In a cavern, in a canyon
Excavating for a mine
Lived a miner, forty-niner
And his daughter Clementine.

Oh my darling, oh my darling
Oh my darling, Clementine
Thou art lost and gone forever
Dreadful sorry, Clementine.

Oh Susanna

An American composer, Stephen Foster, wrote the words and music to this song in 1848.

Allegretto

When you can play the music, try singing the words to "Oh Susanna", or ask someone else to sing along with you.

I came from Alabama with my
  banjo on my knee
I'm going to Louisiana, my true
  love for to see
Oh Susanna!
Don't you cry for me
I'm going to Louisiana
With my banjo on my knee.

It rained all night the day I left,
  the weather it was dry
The sun so hot, I froze to death,
Susanna don't you cry.
Oh Susanna!
Don't you cry for me
I'm going to Louisiana
With my banjo on my knee.

9

Toreador's song

This music is from "Carmen", an opera by a French composer named Georges Bizet. It was first performed in 1875. It is about a woman who falls in love with a bullfighter.

To make "Toreador's song" sound very proud and dignified, play the dotted notes very strictly and don't rush them.

When you know the piece, try it a little faster or a bit slower. Does the mood change when you change the speed?

The trout

The Austrian composer Franz
Schubert wrote this tune around 1817.
Later he used it in a larger piece for
piano and stringed instruments.

Muss i' denn?

The title of this German folk song means "Do I have to?" It is about a man who has to leave his home town. The tune was also used for "Wooden heart", which was sung by Elvis Presley in 1960.

O, du lieber Augustin

This is a very old German folk tune. Its title means "My dear Augustin". In English it is sometimes known as "Buy a broom".

Allegretto

Some friends could help you make this music sound like a German folk band, with the music below. Use recorders, chime bars, or violins (each player should choose the upper or lower note). An accordion or keyboard can play both notes at once. Before you begin playing, count a few bars together so that everybody starts at the same time.

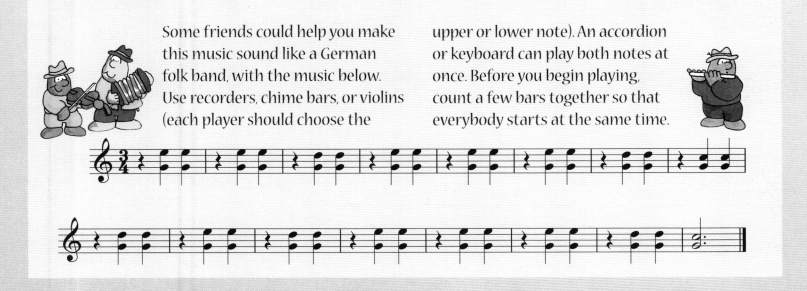

13

Daisy, Daisy

Harry Dacre, an English songwriter, wrote this in 1892. It is about a couple being married and riding away on a tandem (a bicycle for two people).

You could accompany this tune with a drum, shaker or cowbell, using the rhythms on the right. Which one do you like best? Do you like the same one all the way through?

14

Ringing out!

This tune was written specially for this book. When you play it, make a big, confident sound. Someone could play a triangle in time with the long notes.

Take your time!

Ding dong merrily on high

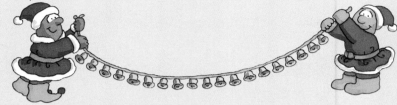

Although this tune is best known as a Christmas carol, it is a French dance from the 16th century.

Try playing the repeated section a few different ways. You could play it quietly the first time then loudly the second. Or begin it quietly and gradually get louder. Can you think of other ways? Which do you like best?

Oh little town of Bethlehem

Nobody knows who wrote this English Christmas carol, but it is hundreds of years old. Play it quietly, like a lullaby.

Andantino

Add the music below on a violin or recorder. (On the violin, it will sound good an octave lower, too.)

Before you begin playing, count a few bars together so that everybody starts at the same time.

Ma oz tsur

Jewish people sing this during Hanukkah, a winter festival. The title means "Rock that shelters me".

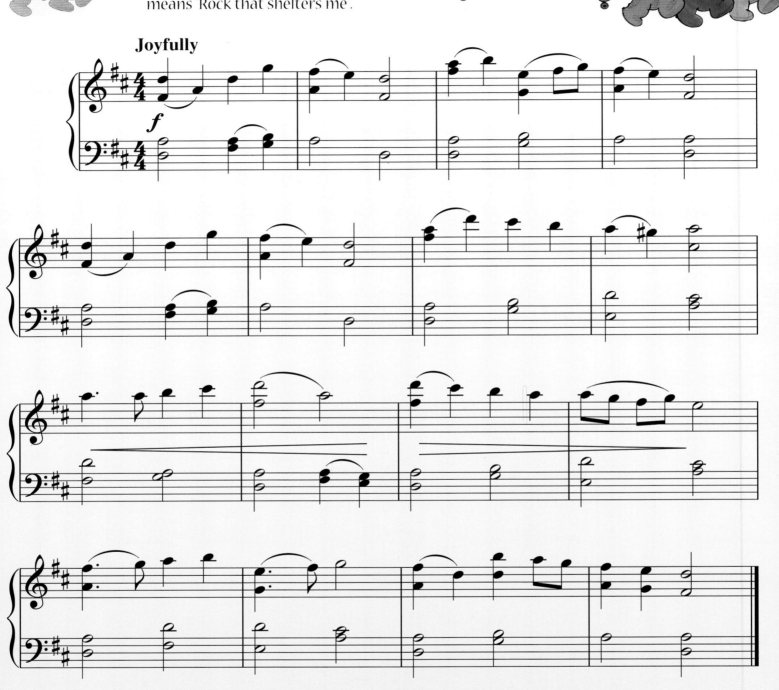

There are signs in the music above to tell you to get louder and quieter bit by bit. The word for getting louder is "crescendo", and the word for getting quieter is "diminuendo". You could try using this effect in other pieces in this book, too.

This sign means "get louder".

This sign means "get quieter".

18

Cockles and mussels

This was written in the 1880s by James Yorkston. It is about Dublin, the capital city of Ireland, and is sometimes known as "Molly Malone".

The Londonderry air

An Irish woman named Jane Ross first wrote this tune down in the 1850s after she heard it played by a local musician.

Slowly and sadly

20

The minstrel boy

Nobody knows who wrote this Irish tune, which is also called "The Moreen". It was first published in the 19th century with words by Thomas Moore.

21

Snake in the grass

This tune was written specially for this book. Can you make it sound very smooth and a little scary? Be careful not to rush the shorter notes.

With a slither

22

Greensleeves

"Greensleeves" was first printed in the 16th century. Some people say King Henry VIII of England wrote it, but this is probably just a legend.

"Greensleeves" is a very old tune, so nobody knows exactly how it sounded when it was written. Once you have learned the music, you can change some of the notes to make other versions. Above the music, you will see some note names in circles. Try playing these instead of the written notes. (You don't have to use all of them. You may like some and not others.)

When you have decided which of them to use, write your version down.

23

Early one morning

"Early one morning" is an old English folk tune. Play the left hand part very smoothly and gently.

Allegretto

24

Waltzing Matilda

"Waltzing Matilda" is an Australian song. It was
written in 1895 by Banjo Patterson, though it is
based on an older Scottish tune called "Craigielee".

Happy birthday to you

The tune to "Happy birthday to you" was written by an American schoolteacher, Mildred Hill, and first published in the 1890s.

If you are singing this song, you need to work out the rhythm of your name in 3/4 time to fit it in to the music. Can you write down the rhythm of your name, or your friends' names?

It may help to clap a steady 3/4 beat and say your name over the top a few times to work out where each part of your name fits.

An - tho - ny

Do - ri

Jen - ni - fer

26

For he's a jolly good fellow

This is an American tune from the
19th century. It is sometimes called
"The bear went over the mountain".

Pause

If you play this at a birthday party, people can join
in. Get them to clap in time with the accented
notes in the second and third lines. Are there
other noises people could make for the accents?
  How long do you think you should hold the pause
in the last line? If you hold it for too long, people
who are singing will run out of breath.

Tingalayo

This tune comes from the Caribbean.
Play the rhythms carefully to make
them neat and precise.

Allegro

Yellow bird

"Yellow bird" is a Jamaican tune. Count the rhythms very carefully and make sure you don't rush the short notes.

Wedding march

A German composer, Felix Mendelssohn, wrote this tune in 1843. Watch out for the repeat.

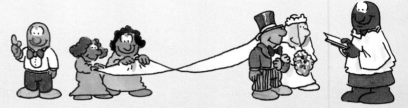

Hymn to joy

A German composer, Ludwig van Beethoven, wrote this tune in 1827. It is now the anthem of the European Union.

Organize a concert for your friends or family. Decide which pieces to play, and in what order. Set a date and a time, and write a list of the music.

Maybe you will want some other musicians to help, either by playing the extra parts that go with some of the pieces, or playing pieces of their own.

31

Notes for teachers

Easy Piano Tunes is an ideal repertoire book for young pianists. It can either be used along with a primer or - with a little explanation from a teacher - on its own. For more advanced pupils, it is an ideal sight-reading resource - it is designed for browsing and entertainment. As well as being fun, the stickers can be used as a progress record and to promote self-assessment.

The pieces are not arranged in strict order of difficulty in the hope that users who browse will find pieces suited to their ability throughout the book. Nevertheless musical and technical concepts are introduced progressively, so that as players work through the pieces they will gradually acquire new skills and develop ones they already have. In particular the pieces are intended to equip young players with the confidence to try new things and to interpret more than just the notes.

Markings such as dynamics are kept to a minimum, and fingerings only inserted where necessary. This is partly to respect the technical abilities of young players, partly to leave room for the teacher's own comments and preferences, and partly to encourage readers to make interpretative decisions of their own.

The book contains three new compositions which explore techniques, sonorities and harmonies that young pupils may not otherwise encounter. On some of the pages there are extra activities which are designed to develop musicianship, to encourage pianists to play with other people and to provide opportunities for transferring skills learned in the piano lesson into the classroom. They also explore some of the challenges pupils will meet both in the aural and musicianship sections of music exams, and in the requirements for music in the school curriculum.

You can listen to all the tunes in this book on the Usborne Quicklinks Website. Go to **www.usborne-quicklinks.com** and enter the keywords "easy piano tunes", then follow the instructions.

First published in 2003 by Usborne Publishing Ltd, Usborne House, 83-85 Saffron Hill, London ECIN 8RT, England.
www.usborne.com